GOD'S VISION

Karen R. Levine

AB **ASPECT Books**
www.ASPECTBooks.com

I had great anxiety, and did not feel any release from this urgency to tell this story—until I started writing it, and making plans to publish it. Why is this story so important? I believe God wants people to know that He is alive; He is not a ghost or a phantom; He is as real as the morning breeze brushing across your face.

He wants to be understood and for "man" that He created to trust and "believe" in Him. He has given us the gift of His son Jesus: He watched Him bleeding, dying, suffering; just so sinful, unworthy man could have redemption. When we think of God—I don't believe we understand that it is painful for Him to watch us sin; to watch us suffer. The consequences of our sins is also painful—death, pain and sickness. When Jesus came to Earth God offered man a solution, a promise, a reassurance that this earthly suffering will one day come to an end. With this promise we have an understanding that "death" is not the end of our lives. We have a second chance to live with our Father forever in paradise— no more sin, death, chaos, sickness; no more pain. Millions of believers carry this promise within their hearts every day. I am one of those believers. In this vision God has left no doubt in my mind that He is real—and that He keeps His promises.

I hope after you read my story it will give you the courage and the strength to change your life; to truly become a believer. Many are often filled with doubt and fear—living their lives thinking there is nothing after death. But that is not true—God's words are true. The greatest gift man can give to God his creator, is to truly believe in Him.

Believing is a choice, the evidence is there—I choose to believe in the promise of God. He has made himself known to me so many times. When I falter and fail, like a loving parent He is there to pick me up and place me back on my feet. God is so loving, patient, and kind—this story is one of my greatest experience with my loving Father. I hope after you read it, it will help you to make the choice to give your life to Him; believe fully, and see how your life will evolve and change. It is one of the greatest gifts you will give to yourself honoring God's purpose for your life.

There are so many courageous men of God in the Bible but I couldn't help but notice Paul. He dedicated his life fervently with such passion and purpose to preaching the gospel; like him, I am hoping that you will take the journey with me— A journey filled with passion, purpose and love for a creator whose love is never ceasing....

This is my story; this is God's vision...

Childhood

My childhood was extraordinarily ordinary, filled with little girl things: such as playing dolls house; and playing "dirty pot" the Jamaican way of saying something very American; "playing with "mud pies. My creative play yielded a handsome husband who would lay beside me at night, helped with the children, and would love and protect me. I played out scene after scene when I wasn't fetching water; or sweeping the dusty yard. Weekend pastimes including playing cricket with my cousins and the children in the village. Braiding the hair of grass dolls would have to wait until Sunday, because Saturday we would spend all day in church. Everyone went to church my aunt, my three cousins, except for my grandmother.

My grandmother's feet could not carry her up the steep mountains so she stayed behind and read her Bible. I remember always seeing her physically frail; carrying her Bible. Her voice was so strong and powerful—it more than made up for the strength she did not have in her legs. She spoke sharply in her native patois, instead of calling my name, she would call me "Pickney" or "gal Pickney" meaning child and girl child— always she spoke so lovingly... The one name she proclaimed day and night was the name of Jesus. I grew up in the bosom of a woman who had embraced God with all her might. She spoke of Him as if He was in the room right beside her. I grew up believing that I could just talk to God because He was alive; He was there.

I asked Him many questions: In the cool of the Jamaican summer nights, I would ask Him countless questions. I imagined Him sitting there beside me answering my questions: I would lay there when the sun was hidden—because I could not look upon the sun. I imagine that God was greater than the sun He created. It made me weep to think that He loved us so much that He would walk with us on Earth and try to teach us things that He knew... I was a little girl contemplating big things.

A curious little seven-year-old girl, laying in the wake of the evening curiously questioning the creator of the universe, how He must have smiled at my innocence: "God do you sleep at night like we do?" "Do you eat? And what is your favorite food? Mine is porridge. I like the way my grandmother makes it. It has more love in it than my aunt's. She yells too much as if she doesn't love me. Over the years, the image of my grandmother stooped down over a make shift stove, to make me the most delicious bowl of corn meal porridge is one that still makes me cry. I knew she loved me because her legs were weak and she was always in pain. And yet still she stooped down stirring that porridge until it was perfect. I imagined that is something like how Jesus loves us—to go through pain; to seek and save the people that were lost.

She always handed me the first bowl of porridge. It made me feel even more special. I believed that my grandmother had Jesus' love inside of her. It made me always wanted to be close to her. I hugged her and kissed her cheeks daily. I could still feel the warmth of her cheeks and my little girl arms around her neck. She used to greet some of my hugs suspiciously:

"Pickney we yu de all morning long?"

I didn't want to tell her that I was exploring through our little village; seeing some lovely mangoes just laying around under a certain neighbor's tree—I decide to help myself. But she could tell because my face was sticky from the juicy mangoes. She looked at me lovingly but had to warn me: "Uffa mango u go tief?"

The question was answered with a tighter hug—"Gramma me never gwan leave you" She smiled knowingly.

Those were my Jamaican days and night a regular little Tom Sawyer; a little girl playing with dolls; climbing trees, trying to keep up with boy cousins who did not always want a girl around. Sometimes I would find myself alone wondering what America was like. My mother had brought me some American apples. The skin was not as soft as our Jamaican apples. In fact I broke a shaky tooth biting into one of them, but I like the way they tasted; different from the usual mangoes with worm surprises. America was a place that stayed in my dreams...

My aunt and grandmother told me the story often of how I came to live with them. My mother suffered greatly; so she handed over a wailing, child to a waiting grandmother's arms. I immediately stopped crying— love had found me. I owe my childhood to my grandmother's love— and a mother from a distance provided for my care...But it was my grandmother's love that had cemented in my heart; a deeper love", one that had taken root; one that had awakened my curiosity to learn more about the power and love of one she never stopped talking about; the one that could walk on water—and created magic with five small loaves of bread and two fishes. I wanted to know more about Jesus. ...A little girl that dreamed big dreams wanted to know about this powerful man who walked with us on Earth and gave His life for us.

The Navel Orange Tree

There was a navel orange tree that stood outside the three room house we lived in. The sun was always directly above the oranges; my grandmother laughed when she gave me the sweet orange slices. She said God had blessed the tree because the sweetness of the fruit made all the people in the village inquired about the tree. I carry the memory of that orange tree even 47 years later.

I was 7 years old when I found myself in the middle of the night under the orange tree in silence. I did not hear any word spoken, just the silence of the dark night—and a peacefulness that I had never felt before. I remember turning around and headed back for the door back to the little bed that I slept by my grandmother's side. I remember waking and telling her about the strangeness of the dream. She became so quiet—then she gave me her Bible—she asked me to read the story of Samuel. And I did in my quiet time, watching the clouds—

I had to talk to God about the dream: Father God, my grandmother thinks that you blessed me under the navel orange tree that give only sweet fruit—she told me to read Samuel. Samuel was older than me; he was 12; I am 7. He was a boy I am a girl. I am not sure what it all means God, but I trust you just like I trust my grand-mother's love... so I feel alright about waking up under the orange tree—I believe you did bless me there. There is something I have to do in this world. I don't know what it is yet...

It seems like the blessing had become a part of me. A noticeable calmness had taken over my spirit so thoroughly. My cousins noticed the change but my aunt said "A give yu till de end of de week". She trusted God but did not trust me. After all-- I was the same overly, active, brash and sassy girl—that she wrote to my mother to come and get me. She told anyone that would listen in her thick Jamaican accent — "And she never tek any telling; own way and hav no manners....

She would describe all the calamities I managed to get myself into like measuring myself against the shortest woman in our village. A woman that was small but had strong enough arms to pull me by my ear up the stony hill to present me in front of my thoroughly aggravated and embarrassed aunt who suggest to the woman that a "good boxing of my ears would set me straight" The woman walked away mad—but was satisfied that I would be punished....

America, 1972

My aunt wrote my mother one of the most urgent of letters: "Come and get yu child...she hav no manners at all—not listening to me..." It was always my mother's intention to take me to America. But I had formed such an inseparable bond with my grandmother—Every time she approached the subject I would cling to my grandmother's leg and pleaded "Me caan't leave my gramma—she need me fe tek care of har" She would smile at me, and teased me with…

"Yu tek care of me?—yu lazy so til…" She laughed her grandmother's laugh—But I knew her heart broke as she watched my little legs descended the rocky hill with my suitcase in hand. She knew that America would hold my future. She stood there and watched me as I disappeared with my mother. I knew it was time for me to go but I also knew as long as she was in this world I would be loved. I felt the peacefulness come over me: I felt this same feeling under the orange tree; a perfect sweet peace. I did not want to lose that feeling—I did not want to leave my grandmother. But I knew that it was time to go to America—besides I couldn't wait to taste the American apples and to see if the streets were really made of gold…

In America

I had watched the lights from the window of the plane. In my eleven-year-old little girls mind, I thought America was a magical place—the sort of place you read about in Fairy Tales. I was surprised to see that America was just as ordinary as the village that I came from in Jamaica. I remember getting up to the smell of chocolate; my mother in her robe—I looked through the sliding glass doors to see a step that went upstairs. We were on the bottom floor of a two story house. The neighbor's children were very noisy.

The place I had come to live in was called Amityville: It reminded me of the small village that I had lived in for eleven years. But the people did not all speak patois and I became quiet and would not speak because my mother expressed that the way

I spoke was "bad." I did not get any hugs from my mother and my cousins were not there to even tease me—I was lonely and afraid. There were children playing outside my bedroom window. But I quietly read my Bible and wished I was home. I now had my own room. My mother had a husband and was planning to buy a house. I thought we now had money since there was a refrigerator, a stove, a nice table to eat from—I had my own room but I missed my grandmother. I occupied my time with wondering if I could find a cure in America for my grandmother's legs.

Suffering and Faith

I had watched my grandmother's "suffering" and "faith" for eleven years—I could understand the "faith" she had but the "suffering" I did not understand. The pain she felt in her legs was sometimes unbearable to watch because she would grimace and make a sound. She went to many doctors but none had the answer as to what caused the crippling pain in her legs—Rheumatoid Arthritis was what one doctor said but there was no relief from the pain—the medicine did not work.

There was some talk of Obeah or Voodoo; the women in the village did not like her because she was not born there—considered a stranger. She was not greeted with open arms. But many people had come to know how kind she was. She took care of so many children—and they came to love her. For people that still hated her she read, Psalm 37. The Bible was like food in our small house. It was life to us. My grandmother quoted the Psalms, especially 23— she came to rely on them for strength and comfort. One time I saw her bent over in such agony—I wondered why

God had not taken the horrible pain away from her legs—we had taken her to every doctor and could not find a source to ease her pain: She had "faith" but still she suffered; for years her situation remained the same. I had sent a letter to my grandmother hoping that my "prayers" from America would help. She wrote back in her grandmother's voice, "Me de ya same way" She said she missed me; she loved me. I already knew those things—what I didn't know is how to find a way to stop the pain in her legs.

I would be like Joseph in a foreign land—the one to save his brothers from hunger. I would save her from suffering. Joseph also suffered but he had faith. God blessed his faithfulness—My grandmother was "faithful" I prayed for her blessings to come: I wanted her legs to be strong; I wanted her to live in a big house; the ones with an antenna on the roof—that would mean she could watch the cartoons that I found so funny like the Flintstones...her legs would not hurt anymore and she would laugh her grandmother's laugh and always be happy. But my grandmother did not want to come to America...

1994

Nothing had changed with my grandmother's legs. I was all grown up, now a woman of 34 years in age. My grandmother still suffered. I wrote telling her that I was pregnant with my third child. The doctor said he would be another boy—I was afraid because my first boy had Autism. So I took extra care resting, and taking my vitamins...With this pregnancy I would

experience something so life chang-
ing that it could not be explained with
the naked eye—the Holy Spirit was
needed to explain what I had seen:

I was pregnant with my last child,
an unexpected joy—only I didn't
know joy then. I was living with a
man; a husband but the smiles were
not consistent like all the "husbands"
I had created playing "dirty pot" in
my little girl dreams: This husband I
did not quite understand—We fought
about everything: his family; and how
to raise my 7-year-old daughter. He
was heavy handed and would not
tolerate any disrespect from her—we
were often yelling and screaming at
each other. Respect was lacking in
our marriage—money was lacking in
our marriage. His nature was secre-
tive, and deceptive. I was always trying to figure out if our relationship
would survive.

December 4, 1994

I started seeing shadows over my head while I try to balance my pregnant belly on the couch. My spirit was troubled: My husband had started a business that was failing—and he was hanging on for dear life. Not heeding the obvious that a baby was coming with only one income; he stubbornly clung to his hopes of retrieving money from a customer. I did not want to fight with him—I had one premature baby already weighing only 2 lbs. 11oz. It was so difficult watching him trying to survive. I asked God to make my baby healthy and strong.

I was not sleeping in bed with my husband that night—my spirit was troubled and I felt trapped in my pregnancy; in our poor way of living. I was seeking God... My thoughts wandered back and forth—I was unhappy and wished I had made better choices in

my life. The shadows were lingering—
something released itself from my
body. I knew that my water broke—
my husband quickly got me to the
hospital—I was bleeding, and there
was an urgency on my doctor's face
when I quickly signed the papers, I
was heading for the operating room...

The surgery had left me weak and
disoriented— when I saw my little
boys face I was happy. He was small
but not as small as my first son. He
weighed 4lbs 11 oz. God had answered
my prayers; my little boy had jaundice
but he was ok—I looked into the eyes
of my beautiful baby; God had blessed
me. He was so helpless—I had to start
feeling stronger so I could take care
of him. But my strength never came
back, even though I was prescribed
iron pills by my doctor who noted the
blood loss in later years by exclaiming
to me in a questionable bedside man-
ner, "You were bleeding like a pig!"

He thinking I was out of harm's way headed for Africa, unknowing that I was about to face the fight of my life...

Life's Blood

I quickly became the woman with the issue of blood...nothing stopped it from flowing—three transfusions and the blood came pouring from my body, collected in buckets for the doctor's observation: The doctors were bewildered as to what was causing this: They checked me for organ damage; and there was none; was the blood being trapped somewhere in my body? They had the information that my doctor left them with— that I had large fibroids: One of them broke; leaving my little boy tangled in the umbilical cord, drowning in blood and fighting for his life. It was a miracle that we were both alive.

I was grateful to God that my son was alive and doing well—but my life had entered the pages of the Bible: I was weak and disoriented; clinging to my Bible literally. My days were spent waiting, waiting, for test results that yielded nothing. Transfusions that left my body cold as ice—Shameful of my bleeding; the woman with the issue of blood hanging on to the garment of one who could heal her. I understood so clearly the suffering of women: I now understood my grandmother's suffering—and clung to my "faith": The only diagnosis I received from the doctors was that I had "severe anemia" the fact that the three transfusions did not stay in my body was still a mystery.

My body was sick, but my spirit had taken on a powerful energy; I could hear everything being said in the hospital from near and far: I heard someone saying, "Some people can die from anemia" I heard my mother's voice coming from the hallway, "Do you think it could be cancer?" Her voice was filled with panic. The sound of every voice lifted up where I could hear every chatter of the doctors, of the people in every room—perfectly clear. Every time I think of how that could be possible—I realize that spirit is so much stronger than death. My blood count kept dropping—but that didn't stop me from being my same sassy self from childhood.

A doctor who had liquor on his breath tried to examine me. Recognizing the poison, I asked that he would not come back in my room—I fell back on my bed as I uttered those words of protest. I could see the comedy in my situation—the passing out, sleeping for hours, then waking up disoriented: I saw my then husband laughing at me; engaging my daughter in mimicking me—it was then I realized that my whole life with this man was a lie and that it surely would not last.

He did not love me, and his "mean-ness" was so apparent in the mimick-ing such a dire situation, when I just gave birth to his child. This peculiar man was laughing but there was not much to laugh at because we were dead broke, no food in the house—no milk for my baby...

In one of my moments of clar-ity I asked the nurse to help me, she brought the social worker in—I called my desperate husband from my sick bed and ask him to go to Catholic Char-ities to put some food in the house. He was only too glad to do it because he was ashamed to ask his family and he could not hide the empty refrigerator from my mother who had arrived only because she heard that the "situation" I was in was not good.

That evening God had provided my family with food—and I was so grateful. I was also grateful that my three children were safe and sound.

My Jen she was only 9 years old; she was worried. I remember trying to put my thoughts together—I had always felt strength in my writing. So I started fighting for my strength. I prayed so hard, just like I've always seen my grandmother do—praying through her suffering: My grandmother never missed a day of prayers. I started talking to God in between the tests, and the discharges home—I did not know what to do...I had a problem with my blood—no doctor had the answer. What kept me alive, kept me talking and walking was nothing short of a miracle itself—one nurse could not believe when she tried to get blood from my veins and got nothing asked me directly, "How are you walking around? There is no blood..."

This alarmed me even more; I kept my faith but I was tired—this kind of tired was like nothing that I have ever felt before. I wanted to sleep but I was afraid I would never wake up—so I started writing to my children:

My first born Jennifer Marie; you are such a beautiful girl: born in such strife—I had not chosen well in the nature of your father but I am glad you are here. My darling daughter, bright, reading at such a young age. Finding salvation in books; you speak of nothing but being a doctor. Stay in school my precious one—don't let anyone disrespect you or take advantage of you. I want so much for you. I love you so much! Don't ever leave school, ask God to guide you…He will be there for you….

I finished my scribbling leaving my body exhausted and I did not know what carried me to make sure my children were alright. I looked at my little one—new born babies are so adorable! I felt such love for him—I wanted to live and see him grow up… I felt helpless but before I fell into self-pity and anxiety I remembered my "faith-ful" grandmother who woke up early each morning to pray. She prayed for all the children that came from her womb...she knew that I was sick and I knew she was on her pain racked knees praying and beseeching God to heal me...

The vision made me laugh out loud: The nurses told me that I slept for three days. I woke up drowsy as if I went on a long journey. I wondered if what I had seen was real or was it just a long dream. I felt like I felt at seven when I found myself in the middle of the night under the navel orange tree reborn, filled with hope, clarity and a sweetness of spirit that cannot be explained with natural words. There were prophets in the Bible that God spoke to but I was not a prophet— what was God trying to tell me through this vision...and what was I going to do with what He had shown me?

The Vision

The sleep I slept was deep: I was at the
core of the universe; lost in the sweetness of my sleep. I woke up to children
beckoning me to come and play with
them. I wanted to drift away but the
children that were playing in a clear,
green meadow were the happiest children that I ever saw. There was a light
shining from their smiles, their hair,
their very being. They were calling

collectively, beckoning "C'mon!" I suddenly wanted to go with them and be a part of them; they were beaming with light and happiness and I wanted to feel that kind of happiness too. The place was green beyond green; life was everywhere—I resisted the tug to go with the children. I remember telling them that I had children of my own to play with. A baby boy newly born would surely miss his mother's arms—but I wanted to stay and be free... By telling them "no" I was transferred to a different place—after watching the children playfully disappearing beyond the sunken hills; their laughter trailing behind them.

There was a light that overwhelmed me until I recognized what it was—I could not look directly into it. But I wasn't frightened by it; it was warm and comforting—I could still hear the laughter of the children but then it stopped as my eyes followed the Pygmy man with white and red painted stripes on his face. Things were moving fast—the Pygmy man moved as he drummed on his drum in a circular motion, repeating the same ritualistic beat; a movement that repeated itself over and over endlessly. I suddenly heard a voice as true as any voice could be; it wasn't loud or soft but perfect; it was perfectly clear: "As a little girl you were always asking me what I looked like.... My eyes suddenly shifted towards a tree that started moving rapidly, through the clouds; beyond the clouds—it kept moving and moving; a tree that had no branches, never stopping. Moving swiftly, upward, continuous, never bending—never ceasing... I wondered how I could see it from where I was, but I could see everything. I was now spirit—spirit so much stronger than death or flesh, kept my eyes on the tree that kept moving, in my mind's eye—it will never stop moving until I past from this Earth.

The voice said pointing to the Pygmy man, "This is man! —and pointing to the tree— and "This is God!..." I understood immediately and started laughing. My laughter made the nurse curious that attended to me—it was such a sweet laughter. She did not know about the sweet, comforting, voice that told me that I would be alright. I did not have to worry; I would see my children grow up; they would find out why my body kept losing the blood that was life sustaining. I had no doubt. A doctor came in and checked me, very frustrated, he says, "What is going on here?" I explained to him how I was feeling about the transfusions that came pouring out of my body—carrying with them, multiple infections...He seems annoyed at all the guesses as to what was wrong with me—and told me that I would be seeing a Dr. Mundia, a blood specialist.

I went to sea Dr. Mundia, who I remembered said out loud, "People are dying from "Hemolytic anemia" — I now had a name to the illness that had plagued me for almost 7 weeks since I gave birth and almost ended my life. My appointment with doctor Mundia was January 24, 1995. Significant in my memory because I had written it down, trying to keep my focused by jotting things down: My equilibrium was off, I could not walk to the elevator on my own, it was as if I was drunk, disoriented, unable to walk by myself—I remember my husband walking with me through the hospital—I did not remember any particular warmness or kindness from him. But I was determined to keep myself up, even though my head felt like a balloon and my feet were wobbling I kept moving.

Perfectly Whole

The last appointment where my (CBC) or blood count was completely normal was 3/14/95. God had completely healed my body from Hemolytic anemia: I now understood what was taking place in my body. I did some research on this form of Anemia—it was described by Hippocrates himself as a corruption of the blood. The red blood cells were going out like broken stars, fading into the dark— they were not replacing themselves. The blood could not sustain itself...

The part that made me curious is that Hemolytic anemia in the ancient Arab world was considered a Jewish minority illness. It could be inherited—I often wondered about my Jewish name—Levine. A Jamaican with a Jewish name. These were not so unusual because the world interchanged people all the time—I laughed even more when I found out that you could also develop this illness by eating Fava beans—I have never eaten a Fava bean in my life. But I knew for certain God had a sense of humor and He was directing my life with this vision. As I got older, the vision haunted me. I realized that God wanted me to share it with the world...and I also wanted to share and explore the dream. What did it all mean a pygmy man; a tree?

Making Sense of the Vision

It took me a long time to write this book what I think God wants us to understand through the Pygmy man which represents mankind is that he is simply made out of dust; predisposed to repeat himself—repeat his sins. Spinning around ritualistic represents man's inclinations to do the same things: Man is both constant and inconstant; you cannot completely depend on him. He still needs his creator to show him "things" that he could not understand on his own—like how a tree can pass through Earth and heaven without ever stopping. The tree represents God: Only God can exist between Earth and heaven, never stopping or ceasing; giving everything he has to both worlds. The children that I saw were brimming with happiness—it brought great comfort to me knowing that they were in such a happy place and were so completely whole—made me accept that death although such a painful part of life is necessary as a conscious separation of Earth and heaven. The Bible says "The wages of sin is death but the gift of God is eternal life" What this means became so clear to me in seeing the smiles on those beautiful, perfect children.

Indeed—it is a vision with the enormous capacity for several interpretations—I thank God that I was honored with the privilege of sharing with you.

Gratitude

I thank Him for sparing my life and allowing me to see my children grow into wonderful, capable human beings—I thank Him for my mother, my aunt, and my heart: my grandmother. With her love and affection, I am always reminded that there is such good in the world…and that God's love is the best love you can have….

The most significant thing that I have learned from this experience is that the God that I talked to as a little girl is so real. He is as gentle as a breeze and more powerful than a storm—but yet He took the time to answer my prayers…to answer my questioning as a little girl. I am in awe of His kindness and goodness towards a world that often is so cruel an unkind. I will always share His love, and his vision. I know it has made a difference in my life—I hope it makes a difference in yours too....

We invite you to view the complete
selection of titles we publish at:

www.ASPECTBooks.com

Please write or email us your praises, reactions, or
thoughts about this or any other book we publish at:

AB ASPECT Books
www.ASPECTBooks.com

11 Quartermaster Circle
Fort Oglethorpe, GA 30742

info@ASPECTBooks.com

ASPECT Books titles may be purchased in bulk for
educational, business, fund-raising, or sales promotional use.
For information, please e-mail:

BulkSales@ASPECTBooks.com

Finally, if you are interested in seeing
your own book in print, please contact us at

publishing@ASPECTBooks.com

We would be happy to review your manuscript for free.